East, Beverley. c.1

Finding Mr. Write.

19.95

DATE			